Advance Praise

"This collection of poems traverses the wilds of pop culture, taking the reader on a ride that is sometimes joyful, sometimes wistful, and always moving. From Taye Diggs to David Attenborough, Marcia Brady to David Hasselhoff, Tager leaves no pop culture stone unturned as he seeks to find the truth behind the pop collections of our lives. If you too would want to 'keep goats and unbridled joy' with you wherever you go, check out *Pop Culture Poetry*."

—Chloe N. Clark, editor-in-chief of *Cotton Xenomorph*

"Tender and ferocious. The Cassius Clay of poets."

—*JMWW*

"Tager grips the livewire of our nostalgia and plays the electric guitar of our hearts. The strings of pop history are plucked, slow and sweet, heavy and fast, shredding us into the little pieces we throw at the feet of our teen idols. As outrageous as the primary texts, Tager mixes bawdy stabs of humor with humility, landing in the fertile grounds of memory, a gentle regret, and a fanboy's joy."

—*Uncharted Mag*

"We fuck with this book hard."

—*Rejection Letters*

Pop Culture

Poetry

The Definitive Collection

by Michael B. Tager

akinoga press

For Megan, the pop in my culture

First edition published by **akinoga press**

Edited, designed, and typeset by mychael zulauf

Cover image: *The Sweet Secret* by Adolf Hering, 1892

ISBN-13: 979-8-9864742-4-3

Poems

Requiem for the Only Idol I've Ever Truly, Deeply Loved

JAN Brady gets me
She's the OG Gen X
(you want latchkeys?
I got twenty)

Benign neglect
is a helluva drug
not even a sonar blip
looked at, but never seen

pleading for love
without the vocabulary
of vulnerability

Marcia
Marcia
Marcia

I always say I'm being funny
but I'm never joking
It's how I disguise truth
cause I don't know how to lie
Jan didn't know either
Jan shot straight
both barrels to the heart
primetime soul-baring

Marcia
Marcia
Marcia

We're not saying
what you think we're saying
That word does not mean
what you think
We're all middle children
We don't always have the language to
expose our breastbones

Here's Jan's Rosetta Stone
Please see me
Please hear me
Please love me

Marcia
Marcia
Marcia

I Am David Attenborough and These Are My Nature Poems

on David Attenborough

Fall, Little Ducklings

for Lil' Bow Wow

THE ducklings, they're falling
from their hidden, rough-grown home
of branches and boughs
What's in the tree-depths?
Piles of egg shells, duck shit
trilled love for brothers and sister ducks
The ducklings, they jump,
hesitation gone like rotary phones
and everyone's innocence
Their downy feathers ruffle
the still breeze,
not contrariwise
Wind can't fuck with ducklings

Me, I'm behind the camera guy
behind the key grip
and I watch the ducklings
tumble to the leafy ground
One day, there will be no forest left
if we continue down this concrete highway

For now, I follow the ducklings down
bounce when they bounce
bounce, bounce with me
Attenborough style
bounce with me bounce with me
bounce with me bounce with me

I Don't Care if You're Six, Seven Feet, a Mile High, I'm David Attenborough

for Bushwick Bill, AKA Dr. Wolfgang Von Bushwickin the Barbarian Mother Funky
Stay High Dollar Billstir

I STAND
beneath a craggy masterpiece
looming through the clouds
a soft nimbus of rain round its peak

I am dwarfed
a Halloween mockery

The crane, it knows theft
it knows terror
I do too. I remember last year
Halloween fell on a weekend
robbing little kids for bags
robbing the night of heaven

This snow topped-corridor
where only goats and lichen dwell
defies me
above oxygen-starved stone crevices
God and Gaea
defy me

I am David Attenborough.
I fear no mountain.
I fear no crane.
I fear no plastic bag.

I approach the mountain and drop those motherfucking B's on em'

the more I swing
the more blood flows

But then it disappears and my best boy disappears too
it isn't even close to Halloween
and I, David Attenborough,
am so tired
of the crumbling peaks

There's a Boaty McBoatface

for Nelly

DO you want to take a ride with me?
See deep denizens in
slow motion capture
capture I command!—behemoths
erupting skyward from placid surface
to feed among the weak and unfit

I ride
Before polyethylene islands
drown the king beneath the waves
the orca with her seaweed crown
the giant squid, suckers a thousand leagues long
the great white is gnashing rage, skin the moon's turned face
draw broken marrow from dark water chasms
you can't see it, unless you skate upon it, a shell beneath your feet
if you wanna take a ride with me, there's a boat, my name writ upon its jib,
writ thereby on water

If you want to take a ride with me, you can
hey. It must be the money
that I've brought to the mother country
to earn a warship, on these
rising tides
of salinity

Run, Motherfucker, or That Cheetah Will Eat Your Entrails

for DMX

THERE, in the distance, the speck, the enigma, the hidden X
moves through Kenyan plains
through high grass, behind trees
stalking, stalking, stalking
gazelle! I implore you! Channel me
break bread with the enemy
but no matter how many cats I break bread with
I'll break who you sending me.

It is clear now, when we zoom in
our eyes the window to nature's world
gazelle! I implore you as the cheetah approaches, channel me
first we gonna rock
then we gonna roll
then we let it pop, go let it go!

Run, gazelle
The X marks your tender underbelly
cheetah's breath upon your tail
feel it draw near

I put in work, and it's all for the kids
but these cats done forgot what work is
you can sprint away, you can outlast
if only you stay with the herd

As its claws dig your flank, hot mouth hunting your hidden loins
realize this:
X gon give it to ya. He's gon give it to ya.

Xenomorphs, No. Birds of Paradise, Yes.

for 2pac

I ATTENDED this party
at Beverly D'Angelo's house
not long ago
in the hills surrounding the city of angels
she was once an actress
In her sitting room, beside the divan
perched a bird of paradise
I sat beside this bird.
at the party
in the hills surrounding the city of angels
California, it does know how to party

At this party, outside a city—
not Compton. The other one—
this bird of paradise
showed me its tail feathers
it danced for me
it danced for the world
it danced to burn the world to the ground
hoping beyond hope,
that those that let it ride
would arrive

There are no mates for you, I told this bird of paradise
this poor, widowed chartreuse delight
and I heard a voice
at this party, in the hills surrounding the city of angels

"Who even are you?"

It was Sigourney Weaver

(she was in Alien Resurrection)

(she dubbed Planet Earth for the Americans)

(why did America replace me?)

(Didn't they see Alien Resurrection?)

I said,

"picture me rolling"

Within the Humble Earth Stand I, David Attenborough, Vampire Lord

for Missy Elliott

STALACTITES drip drip drip
onto my shoulders
I scream
David Attenborough doesn't do the damp
I can't stand the rain
I'm a supa dupa fly

Out of the musty shadows
come the squeaking hordes of Zarathustra
of the Impaler
and of Cthulu
guano-infested denizens of dark dungeons
they twirl around me, an inky halo
nip nip nip!
They draw blood
and strength courses
even as I crumble to my knees

Camera-man and boom operator scream their death throes
death of a thousand bat cuts
I sleep
when the rain hits my windowed soul
I take and inhale, cough me some endo
sway on dosie-do like you loco
my devil power surges
and I crave the night unspoilt
fangs' growth uninhibited
by earth's crust above me, below me

Blood, I will drink

when I tread upon dewy grasses again

curled in my toes

I will find casual weekend warriors

I will knock on the windows of their vehicles.

beep beep, who got the keys to the jeep?

Vroom.

Polar Bear Co-Pilot

on Björk

All Neon Like

MCDONALD'S signs in the Apocalypse

what would that look like?

Would the bombs falling

affect the 100% beef patties?

I don't know

I can't sleep

Please tell me

A Boy, Venus

A THOUGHT experiment
what if potato was pronounced camel?
(Wait, no, that's not what I mean)

What if marmalade was more
than just fancy jam?

What if requests for privacy
were respected with wise nods
instead of baby carriage camera intrusions
and ass whupping rectification?

Let me rephrase
because control groups are for suckers
mistaking science for steeples

Violent, Happy

I NEED my leader to feed me happiness
in a gold lamé song
and dresses made of swan
Baton twirlers with rainbow stripes and blood-red teeth
inspire chin checking dance numbers
set to vaudevillian music box

We all need mentors
we all need co-pilots

Isobel moves
from bucolic foliage
to angry concrete
sublime street peddlers
rhapsody in chain link is impossible
when bus rides and office chairs fatten thighs
stars draped in gaslight

I believe nothing
if idols don't tell me

Shh

VALLEYS and mineshafts
lurk beneath
your skin
I can't fathom the
synthesizer black hole wellsprings
these pores opening to your soul

It's not the language barrier,
grunts and whistles are common tongue
and your English is impeccable
I can't avoid double negatives

Inexplicability is
a wood-burning stove under your clavicle and
I relish misunderstanding

What's the opposite of alarm?

Musicals

WE need more song and dance numbers
to celebrate high school graduations
or sexy time

What if we used the world as canvas
car horns as acrylic ink
tangos as retirement parties?

We'd be happier at funerals and first birthdays

Just because it's obvious
doesn't mean I'm wrong

Slow-Ballad

I DON'T keep cutlery
on mountaintops
The mass and velocity of
spoons, falling from cumulonimbus
is probably an equation,
but math and science aren't the point

The summit of Mt. Everest
is littered with detritus
from folks just like me:
unremembered femurs
empty oxygen tanks

I'd keep goats and
unbridled joy up there with me
and the whipping wind

That's freedom

Champion of My Heart

on Taye Diggs

Brown Sugar

I FIRST saw your sensitive glasses
and beautiful bald head
in *Brown Sugar*
a film about
hip-hop and love
You spoke of the Beastie Boys
but I knew you cared nothing for Paul Revere
only for my burgeoning
bulging
heart,
full of you

No sleep
till us

Rent

TAYE, when I tell people
I love you,
I don't mean metaphorically
I mean, I love you like I love
my wife
I want to run my callused hands along your smooth skin
whisper into your ear
my hot springs breath steaming
your vacation-home beauty

It's not gay
when it's you

We're all Taye-Sexual
when our skin is flayed
and our souls burst with song shrapnel

Not America's Top Model

SOMEONE asked me
if Taye Diggs was in this reality show
about crazy half-children
trying to be famous
and I said, "No.
His eyes shatter television screens.
with crystal purity."

"Not all beautiful black men
with poetry hearts
and falcon wings
look the same."

But it turned out
it was you

The Best Man

I AM already married
my brother was my best man
but I watched your movie
and you were a writer
with sensitive glasses
(which I get)
If I did it again
I'd drape you in white satin
and appoint you best man of everything
the costume changes
would be worth it
because you are my soul

Scott Leo

I DON'T care that Taye is not your real name

I still want you elbow-deep inside me

because your heart is go! go! gold

and your teeth are an orchard of sunflowers

an ocean of fractured, molten glass

a dubloon-filled dungeon

in my sparrow heart, you are Taye

not Scott Leo

and I love you

Lucy Liu is Beautiful and That's My Problem, Not Hers

on Lucy Liu

Virginity

MY first time was with a woman who
resembled Lucy Liu
First times set precedent
ice-skating skinned knees
sour-apple surprise
fist pump purple sky

Even the good ones
leave scars to protect
exit points from corruptive air

Safeguard my pillow heart
that still loves
a bottom-tier Bond flick
and melancholic first times

Lucy Liu will never die
not for me

Can't Talk. On Drugs.

I'VE never seen Lucy Liu
unawesome. I'm not judging her
talent or agent or whatever
It's not normally my place to quantify spirit
no one asked for my two bits but pop
culture is public domain
I have questions
I have hot takes

Lucy Liu is mostly acid,
usually deadpool jokes and threats
and I want to see deep cut Liu
I want rom-com and seven-layer chalupa renditions
of the *Tempest*
I crave her bombed-on-benzos in a biopic based on my life
the time I dropped acid and crashed a toddler's birthday
emerging from the woods all yeti'd
"You want some cake?" we're asked
"Can't talk. On drugs." we say

She'd be better at my life than I ever am
She'd be prettier even though glamour is only an eighth of the equation
We're nothing but human sketches over viscera
and birthday cakes are lies
I want more from the world than what I'm given

Silvermist?

FRIENDS, countrymen
this is a mortar shell public service announcement
lobbed into your sitting rooms:
there's a series of Tinkerbell movies
(co)starring Lucy Liu

Direct-to-video
operates on its own alternate timeline
hurts no one
brings joy to clapping, tasteless children

Pretty rad.
There's a wonder in discovering
what I've missed even if it's
probably terrible
like half of Liu's filmography

I don't need to own everything

The tag line:
"Enter the land of Tinker Bell and her four best fairy friends."
God, that sounds stupid

Or does it?

Charlie's Angel

I SAW *Charlie's Angels*
not the feathered
hair of Fawcett
and no, it's not good
but it's not as bad as punching myself
in the face
It's a tiny terror
a shoddy special sauce
not an apocalypse
but even so

If a tree falls
and the beholder is an asshole
who cares about sound?

Yasumi Will Rock You

on Yasumi Matsuno

The Rhyan

AFTER liberation who cleans
sands of blood?
Who buries the hawkmen?

Do they roast the hellhounds
and wear mermaid-scale necklaces?
Do the paladins and
evil ones receive PTSD services?

Under the water
do the crabs feast
on drowned amazons
and sunken gryphons
their feathers matted?

Our modern-now games and fables
leave that out
just like they don't show
the detritus of Normandy

War is easy
three steps removed

Let Us Cling

I ROLEPLAY avatars
of just and good
(sometimes grey on grey on grey)
Don't stop me now
I'm out for justice

role-evil-play ain't my jam
There's no room
for death and destruction in my fantasy

The venal is ever-present
the shit of our soul-chakras
When propositioned
with the way of the closed fist
character bonuses
and unique companions if I
stab and slash the weak
it's a hard pass

Who are they fooling?

I can't stand the guilt
I can't stomach
even fake-slaughter
and midi-screams

Ogre

QUEEN—Freddie and Brian and them—
inspires nothing in me
The split pea soup of rock and roll

Yasumi Matsuno hears Queen
and creates detailed histories of imagined worlds
Angel jihadists, overlords of sickly evil
liberation Armies of vengeful men
Stones of power—how the fuck do they work?
The whys of MacGuffins ain't important
it only matters that they matter

Sonic Youth's first album sold one thousand copies
and every one of the buyers
tricked out their garages with basses and amps,
maybe some keytars
(that's hyperbole)
Only twenty-five thousand people bought Yasumi's SRPG
and at least one of them
is now an artist

To my credit,
I play Yasumi's dreamscape and write poems
about Mages and Liches
and the rings in between
So maybe inspiration is dry lightning

The right spark, the wrong time
a grassfire set
from heavy wind

March of the Black

WHEN I was 14
I played *March of the Black Queen*
expecting Zen escape

I wasn't a black-swathed pretend-depressive
just mediocre
and slogging through haunted swamps

It's a metaphor. Swamps = angst
it's not just a day at the races
It was
my first rodeo

Yasmui incorporated bones
and slime and devils
Hunted refugees
murdered to death
Not even sub-
It's all text

Yasumi allegoried
the Yugoslav genocide
in video game orchestra
Flutes and clerics' ankhs
inspired by Mercury's Rhapsody

It's not argyle, but it is a pattern
a conscious attention
to darkness

It's better to shine light on the devil

we process stories better

than literal truth

An apple isn't an apple until it's parallel

to a carbon copy of itself

Only then can we put it in our mouth

Sin-eaters all

Tactics

MATSUNO created
3 chapters in a universe book
and then was called up
to the Major Leagues
Instead he dipped out of for pastures of gold
I can't blame him

It's not that I'm unhappy
playing Double-A
my king-pawn sepsis strike
is to wait and work
and build my own playground
but

would I leave for the right price?
I mean, sure
I'd just haggle

Matsuno,
can you finish your world-building?
I can't stand not knowing
the final chorus
a little silhouette of a man

Do the fandango
drop dragon napalm
Nothing really matters
until the battle-dance ends

I'm a Belieber

on Justin Bieber

Justin Bieber, as Dalmatian

ARE you skittish? Are you too big
for your own good?
Too pretty?

Folks want to wear your skin
a tattooed coat
dewy with hydrated fame

I think it's creepy
I know your spots change color with the solar
wind. I'm aware your hips are bear traps
your ears filled with songbirds
You are no housedog
You belong outside
grinning in the summer rain

Justin Bieber, as Opossum

YOUR pouch is full
of young fans
creeping on middle age

You can't succor them
you have no teats
Besides, who nurses you?
Are you alone in the wind
when the demons float through?

Climb that sycamore,
from the terraced landscape
Dig your own burrow
and eat them grubs
Grow full and fat
with babies

Justin Bieber, as Clownfish

CAN we all
stop dragging the Biebs?
His music is fine
his dancing, the same

(Usher showed him the ropes
the ropes showed him Usher)

The Biebs burns like mouthwash
and glows with winter
I'm full of it
Full of him

I'm a Belieber

Justin Bieber, as Plantain

I'D probably eat you
fried deeply enough
You'd taste like riches
and too-early fame
A little damaged
a little too ripe
Like Kalamata olives

Our bodies are stardust and stardust
is space dirt
and space dirt can't rock my palate
without loads of basil
and a pinch of happiness

I'm a unique star, too
I'd taste like slow pork
We'd go well together
with some jerk seasoning

Justin Bieber, as Broken Child Celebrity

I WOULD never want
child star glory for anyone
They won't love your teddy bear heart
after you outgrow the cute
when you shamble,
covered in lint and dust
full grown, a grey-hearted adult

They should love your safety deposit box chest.
You saw some shit
with too-tender skin
hiding too-tender organs
and too-tender blood

I too would cover my body in black ink
in your spotlighted easy chair

Sorry dude. Better luck
next time

Justin Bieber, as Forgotten Titan

PLEASE, Lord of Mountains
and Twilight
your breeches of fire
and triple mouths scare me

Don't hurt me
Bieber, please

The smoke comes from inside the house
and carries youth through
the chimney

The city is barred
but still you escape
unleashed from Earth's mantle

Who hurt you, my bud?
(sike! I know
it's everyone)

I'm sorry
Want a hug?

Justin Bieber, as Dead and Blasted City

IHOP still stands

It's a lonely kid at a playground
rocking a one-sided seesaw
A Dollar General winks in the distance,
A husked-out Bagel, Bagel
beckons besides a cave of a dance studio

Ain't no parties up in here, up in here

Where's my house?
Where's my summer camp?
All my friends are dead,
or blasted on pills and Maker's Mark

The rats are mutated,
third eyes and five wings
Ghouls roaming the dumpsters feasting
on radiation

I'm just lost and sad
a little maudlin from everything
It's a bad trip and there's no end in sight
not when roaches inherit my terracotta water pipes
and chew my treasured memories

Mr. Bieber, will you
write a banger
to forgive this moment

Justin Bieber, as Capitalism

YOUTUBE was free before
you were a big deal
Ads and paywalls came
after we were hooked on you,
our sweet,Canadian heroin

That's how they get ya
First one's free

The inflation of pop stars means
a dollar buys less of your time

The brightest firefly burns
a Zephyr dream,
but only at-cost
I have the money, I just can't justify
spending it on you

Tao of Swayze

on Patrick Swayze

Dirty Dancing

HE'S not like anything
he is the sky, the double-breasted mullet suit
a shadowy corner savior
tolerating no
exiled babies

He is the oak tree of my heart, the strawberry
shortcake of success
He is the wind
gently blowing
his own perfect locks

Swayze

Point Break

THERE'S a place where points
break and lightning
laden with crystal bullets
crash to the earth.
Where Reagan's rubber neck and
diamond eyes pierce my flakjacket soul
Where Gary Busey dies and it's a
tragedy beyond death
beyond sandy-beach toxins

Beyond Swayze

Roadhouse

I AM not famous
a Nietzsche-spouting bouncer
treasure digging throat-holes
with perfect palm flash
I am not
a mulleted delight
living in Spartan carriage lofts
of Tai chi dignity

There is only one
Swayze.

Ghost

GHOSTS of today and of tomorrow
ghosts of perfection
of marmalade and naked Sundays
We could be ghosts of steamy clay melodies
chained or otherwise
Only a few, the lucky, the beautiful
can be ghosts

of Swayze

Ghost Stories

Marilyn Haunting

MARILYN wakes
eats corn flakes from a
chipped ceramic bowl in
a bougie mansion's abandoned kitchen

Marilyn sings into the void
claws her hair
into ringlets of ice
She knows she blazes

Marilyn waves on the way to the grocery store
wings it every day
Homeless undead, no PO Box
She follows a retiree from the produce section
sits shotgun, sings along to Patsy Cline

Marilyn takes Ambien with ethereal fingers
watches Law & Order
over old folks' fragile shoulders
She sparkles at every solved mystery

Marilyn sleeps on a sofa, dreaming
Praying to the sun and moon and to Death
(clearly on sabbatical)

Marilyn wakes
eats oatmeal
in the kitchen; "Hi I'm Norma, hello hello"
and they only see the wall through her ribcage

Genghis Sees a Michael Bay Movie

HE sits in
an empty handicapped seat
ectoplasm mingling with
calcified Jujyfruits
ready for true, Michal Bay cinema
He's been dead so long
he forgets what having a body is.

He adjusts his leather codpiece
—millennia out of fashion—
and the previews engulf his ghostly ennui
until a piece of popcorn
then toss Milk Duds, Sour Patch Kids
plummets through his gossamer head
and whispered giggles float
through the plush seat
cushions.

Genghis, they call,
go fuck yourself

Genghis concocts lemon-scented fantasies:
casual hatred stored in their spleens
seeps into his soul
He's dead, not invulnerable to scorn
He once asked forgiveness
from a long-dead peasant woman
with tiny feet and
a hole where her heart used to be

"It's been a thousand thousand
sunrises and I'm nothing but dust
and the descendants of worms
Isn't that enough?"

"You might be featured in
Budweiser commercials, but you broke
the world," the peasant woman said
"Time passing doesn't settle graves."

The movie begins
but the barrage does not stop
We remember you, they shout
even if time painted you beige

The movie ends in fractal explosions
Genghis exits into the night, heckled and pelted

John Ritter Is Already Forgotten

HE might as well be

a poor

None of his reruns are streaming

His time share

has power

and the waves outside the floor-to-ceiling windows

never cease their chatter

He plays the TV endlessly

Skip-skip-skipping channels

It's endless being dead

The mirror is empty space

He just wants to see his apple-smile

that minted his fortune

one last time

on his way out

whenever that is

Please. Come and knock.

Please. Come and knock.

Stephen Hawking Bathes in the Glow of a Dying Star

IN space,
no one can hear you scream
with joy
at the liberation from the mortal coil
and the jet streams
of neutrons
that goose your netherly nethers

Whoop with child delight
Ride your phantom wheelchair
along the event horizon
of deathly half-life
A surfer galactic
The cosmos has other plans
You don't mind not being an insider

There are other deathforms out here:
sentient crystallized trees
hydrogen-based evangelists
dancing in a gravity well
God's drumbeats vibrate
their chalk outlines

Stephen Hawking
is where he's always belonged
straight chilling

Underrated

on Whoopi Goldberg

Uhura / Guinan

YOUR role model
wasn't no maid
though she wore short skirts,
tight round black thighs

When you were a woman
a constellation
you gave homage
with overwrought, muffin headwear
and a ludicrous backstory

The Nexus?
Please.

Squares

BORN Caryn Johnson
you gave yourself
a Semitic surname
because adversity didn't
scare you
and because passing
wind is peaceful
like the grave
Whoopi

Purple

WHEN snark is gone
what is left? Only
a glitterstorm
windmill of paint
and admiration
Zingers doper
than sunburnt giants
and worse than your film
with Oprah

EGOT

YOU'RE in rare company
Your mantel supports
the megaphone and the angel
twin faces of drama
the serious man
You, Whoopi,
are the EGOT

That's nothing to my hero-worship
I would build a bronze bust
on my front lawn
of your grin
your locks
among the magnolia

View

IF I watched daytime
talk shows, or if their reruns played
in the twilight hours, when I can't sleep
I would watch *The View*.

Maybe you've lost all the shits
you had to give
like dropping weight
or divorcing toxic friends
to cleanse your tired soul

But maybe it has
merit, if you're involved

Better Than You

FORGET imagery
I say this plain
and leave out the front door

You are better
than the suits
responsible
for *Sister Act 2*

Cycle of the Hoff

on David Hasselhoff

found poetry curated from
The Very Best of David Hasselhoff Amazon reviews

Human Fighter jet

SECONDS after
pressing play on
"The very best of David Hasselhoff" CD
i turned into a human fighter jet and flew
into the sun.

Searching for meaning—and finding it

I JUST typed "Hasselhoff"
into an online
German-English translator
and you know what came up?
"Hasselhoff".

I'm glad you're back in my life, David!

I ONCE stupidly thought
that David Hasselhoff
'only' saved lives
in the choppy yet warm waters
of California

Who's all musicy?

WHEN I listened to this CD
my pants flew
around the room and
promptly landed in a position
resembling that of either
and aardvark or
an oscelot
I'm not sure which
since I
am not
a zoologist.

Perfectly Perfect

HOLLY. Presley. Lennon.

Bolan. Hendrix. Morrison. Cobain.

Hasselhoff.

Why do the good die young?

A K-pop Universe

for Mandy May

BLACKPINK Is the Moon

THE moon dances and
speaks in Korean, English,
all the love languages of bone

Jisoo is the Sea of Tranquility
and Jenni is the Lake of Summer
Hey moon
Whistle

The moon has all the dope pop-and-locks
& choreographed waltzes
Poets see the moon's cratered heart
Poets know how to match the moon's
sick moves

Rose is the Bay of Love
Lisa is the Blue Area
Hey moon
Whistle

Every person I've loved
has Luna ringtone
BLACKPINK is the moon

Hey moon
Whistle

BTS Are Now Exiting the Heliosphere

THE Bang-Tang Boys
are too pure, too good
too beautiful to be owned
They can't live here anymore
They belong to the stars

Voyager carries relics of our story:
Humanity's Rosetta Stone
What's the point?
All we need is Rap Monster and the squad
on a carbonite spaceship
They're dynamite, TNT
They're boys with love

The aliens would get what we're putting down
They'd welcome us
with open bio-carbon tentacle filaments
They're pre-drafted
into our BTS Army

Somewhere in Heaven, Girls Day Has Reunited

AT a certain distance
everything is hypothetical
even with a Hubble
and advanced math.
It's just a thought experiment
How can we believe in the Oort Cloud
if we die
before our fingertips caress?

Poets understand death better
The impossible is poem fodder
Science is salad dressing
Poets don't care what's real
they just write with more of the magic
painted in their nails

My poetry is a spacewalk handstand
I'd tape a disc man to my helmet
and bump Girls Day for the cosmos
Analogue is best for space jams
The Moon Men have yet to hear anything so good
If they yell loud enough
across the void
Girls Day will hear
and get back together for one part

Without gravity,
could I see past Pluto
into Heaven?

Maybe in the Oort Cloud
I'd find all the poets who loved
so fiercely it killed them

Europa Is the Best Heavenly Body and It's Not Even Close

I DON'T understand boredom
There's mystery everywhere
Infinite question-parties and
me in my birthday hat
ready for answers wrapped
as presents

Which is the best moon
and why is it Europa?
Which competition-based reality show produced
the best band, and why is it the Pussycat Dolls?
(Momoland is a hard second)
Bboom bboom!

I know enough about the universe
to realize I'm a dumb asshole
On a bell curve, I'm 3rd from the right
too aware of my limitations
too ravenous for answers, like
why did Momoland fall from grace like that? or
is there life hidden
in Europa's ocean belly?
Bboom Bboom?

Consider this rhetoric my gift
a box of anti-lamentation
Do you know the configuration?
Does Momoland?
Does Europa?

Ask me your tough questions
I'll look into your abyss
lean in, mouth gaping, eyes a-flutterbye
You minx. You
enigma. I'm in love with mysteries
and anything truly loved is immortal
remains inexplicable

Baam!

Golden Girls Special

on The Golden Girls

Something Golden

THERE'S a house
in the swampland
where the girls—oh
the girls!—give praise
to one another, to time,
to the sun

The world remembers
the girls—oh the girls—
celebrating small adventures
small loves
massive hearts
free, from it all

The girls of gold
mother and daughter and
sisters-not-by-blood
We give thanks
to the girls—oh the girls—
for being our friend
down
the road & back
again

Rose

GIRL, when you
were golden
you smelled so sweet
I could lick your sweat

You're still a Betty,
distracted by shiny metal
and reflected starlight
You absorb heat
and exhale sunfire sonnets
you silly goose

I'd give my ribs
for high tea with you
to slap five
with those old hands
wrinkled and wise

A bygone era
didn't pass you by
You passed it

Dorothy

GIRL, I'm not calling collect
You're here, tall & proud & sassyjaded
A voice of cynical reason
A timbre I learned from you

The distance between now and then, me
and you, is way shortened
You're the only one who knew your shit
too aware to be truly happy

Look at Dorothy
Look closer than you think possible
Drink her in
Smell her soul
Dorothy is you
Dorothy is me
Dorothy is all of us for
better and worse

Sophia

GIRL, growing old
isn't so bad
Shadows grow longer as the days refuse to
concede. You're amongst friends, daughters,
soul sisters. Gitchie, gitchie, ya-ya, da-da

It's not that you like Florida
you just like death less
Life at the Equator has its
advantages. Your fingers burn less
and your dreams spawn all the beautiful boys
you knew generations ago
They still love you there
You haven't forgotten them
Voulez-vous coucher avec moi ce soir?
You've still got it
You never lost it
You're not sour, you know
You're not truly mean
You only know the joie de vivre that
taking the piss is
Life's a joke and you're here
for the laugh track
You aim to go down swinging
in the last years
you have left
Au revoir les enfants

Blanche

all lines taken from *Golden Girls* scripts

NOBODY ever believes me when
I'm telling the truth
I guess it is the curse

Flirting is part of my heritage
I got arrested at
a party in Chattanooga because
I mixed a margarita
in a sailor's mouth
I was upset
that I was not the center of attention

Isn't it amazing?
My toe is on the line
I feel so bad
I look so good
If you'll excuse me I'll
take a nice hot, steamy—

what am I doing here?
I feel like the middle of an awful dream
get the net
treat my body like a temple

I am shocked
It's not pertinent at the moment
I want details
I have no secrets
God, I wish
I was dead

Acknowledgements

THANKS to all the editors at the wonderful journals who published these pieces in various forms: *HAD, Longleaf Review, Ligeia Magazine, Rejection Letters, Breadcrumbs, Welter, Skelter*, & *Babe Press*. Some of these presses are defunct, but I still love them.

Ian Anderson, who published these under his nascent press, Mason Jar, deserves and is getting some thanks. (Thanks!)

Tracy Dimond, Adam Robinson and Amanda McCormick A) showed me poetry in such a way that I could finally get it, B) taught me what poetry could be and C) made me own my own poetry. Thanks y'all.

My publisher, mychael zulauf, deserves copious thanks for this as well. It wouldn't exist without him. Thanks thanks thanks!

Finally, thanks to Megan, for supporting me every day.

(I wanted to thank everyone, but that's impractical and I would definitely have left someone important out, so I decided not to try. Sorry! Also not sorry!)

Bio

MICHAEL B. TAGER is a writer and publisher from Baltimore. He is the managing editor of Mason Jar Press and the author of *Pop Culture Poetry: The Definitive Collection*. He doesn't much care for cucumbers, the works of Charlotte Bronte, nostalgia, or the Oxford Comma. He adores Colin Firth, *Tokyo Drift*, and BLACKPINK. His work has been published widely, but not extremely so.

other titles from akinoga press

find more at akinogapress.com

TOUCH / breaks
poetry chapbook by Dina Paulson

Women and Other Angels
poetry chapbook by Kelly Burke

112th Street Notebook
poetic suite by Kristjana Gunnars

An Essential Melancholy
full-length poetry collection by Lora Robinson

Healing Where You Are: an Introduction to Urban Foraging
practical guide to urban foraging by Suzannah Kolbeck
with illustrations by Kim Mattison

Double Exposure
poetry chapbook by Maria C. Goodson

The Candle Moth
prose poem by Dave K

ACREAGE
poetry collection by Stephanie Garon

Plant Power Sisterhood: an anthology of eco-revolution
anthology of Indigenous eco-writing edited by Jenny Fraser

NADIA
sensuella (sensual novella) by mary adelle